A LITTLE CURRENCY

Brazil, Ghana, Japan, Mexico, Switzerland

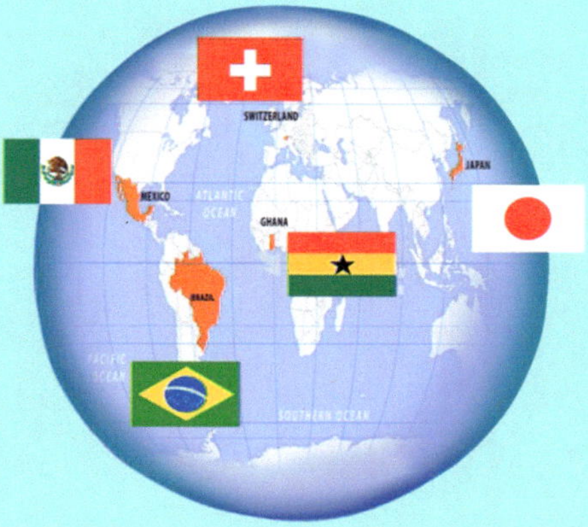

By: J. Mobley

Illustrated by: Indalecio Chavez Jr.

This book belongs to:

____

Country Name and Flag

Mexico

Brazil

Japan

Ghana

Switzerland

Currency Name and Symbol

Mexican Peso	₱
Brazilian Real	R$
Japanese Yen	¥
Ghanaian Cedi	₵
Swiss Franc	₣

Currency pronunciations are noted with an (*)

All around the world,
money has different faces,
and it looks very different,
when in different places.

Money can be red,
orange, blue or green,
and may show famous faces,
like presidents, kings or queens.

SWITZERLAND
JAPAN
MEXICO
ATLANTIC OCEAN
GHANA
PACIFIC OCEAN
INDIAN OCEAN
BRAZIL
PACIFIC
SOUTHERN OCEAN

Every country uses money
and it is not all the same you see.
Money can have different names,
but we call it all currency.

Banco de México
100
Cien Pesos
X2474813
REPÚBLICA FEDERATIVA DO BRASIL
1
BANCO CENTRAL DO BRASIL
REAL
A 0054078790 C
1000
日本銀行券
千円
AB717062J
FEDERAL RESERVE NOTE
THE UNITED STATES OF AMERICA
ONE DOLLAR
BANK OF
GHANA
₵1
JP0265466
One Cedi
10
SCHWEIZERISCHE NATIONALBANK
BANCA NAZIUNALA SVIZRA

Mexican Peso (₱)

Each time we go to Mexico, we spend the Mexican Peso. Use it to visit the Aztec ruins, and buy tacos and nachos with queso.

*Pronounced: "pei-sow"

Brazilian Real (R$)

**The Real is the money
that we use
in the country Brazil.
Visit the beaches
and the Amazon rainforest,
then samba
and have a good meal.**

***Pronounced: "ree-al"**

Japanese Yen (¥)

**The Yen is currency of Japan,
spend it whenever you go.
Buy a ticket for the bullet train
from Osaka to Tokyo.**

*Pronounced: "yen"

Ghana Cedi (₵)

If you trade gold in Ghana,
the Cedi is the currency you earn.
On your first visit go to Accra
and try the cocoa when you return.

***Pronounced: "see-dee"**

Swiss Franc (₣)

**When we ski in the Alps
of Switzerland
we use the Swiss Franc
to save and spend.**

*Pronounced: "frank"

Goodbye for now,
but come back soon,
to learn more about currency.

Next time we will cover
other kinds of money
and travel to new countries.

See you next time

About the Author

Johnnie Mobley Jr., MBA, CPA, PMP

Author J. Mobley (Johnnie Mobley Jr.) is an accountant, consultant and professor. He holds degrees from Pepperdine University and the University of Washington. J. Mobley has worked in accounting and finance for more than 10 years with Fortune 500 companies, small businesses and governmental organizations. J. Mobley writes books to help others by promoting financial literacy and business efficiency.

J. Mobley uses rhyme and visual examples to explain financial concepts. J. Mobley speaks to kids and community organizations to promote understanding of finance and money. When he isn't working, J. Mobley can be found with his family.

J. Mobley published his first book, "A Little Accounting" in 2019 which was met with immediate success, selling in multiple countries around the world.

Products and info can be found online at:

www.alittleaccounting.com

Follow us on Twitter @Accounting4kids

A LITTLE ACCOUNTING
By J. Mobley
Illustrated by Ishika Sharma

Made in the USA
Monee, IL
05 November 2026

67378009R00017

A LITTLE CURRENCY

Brazil, Ghana, Japan, Mexico, Switzerland

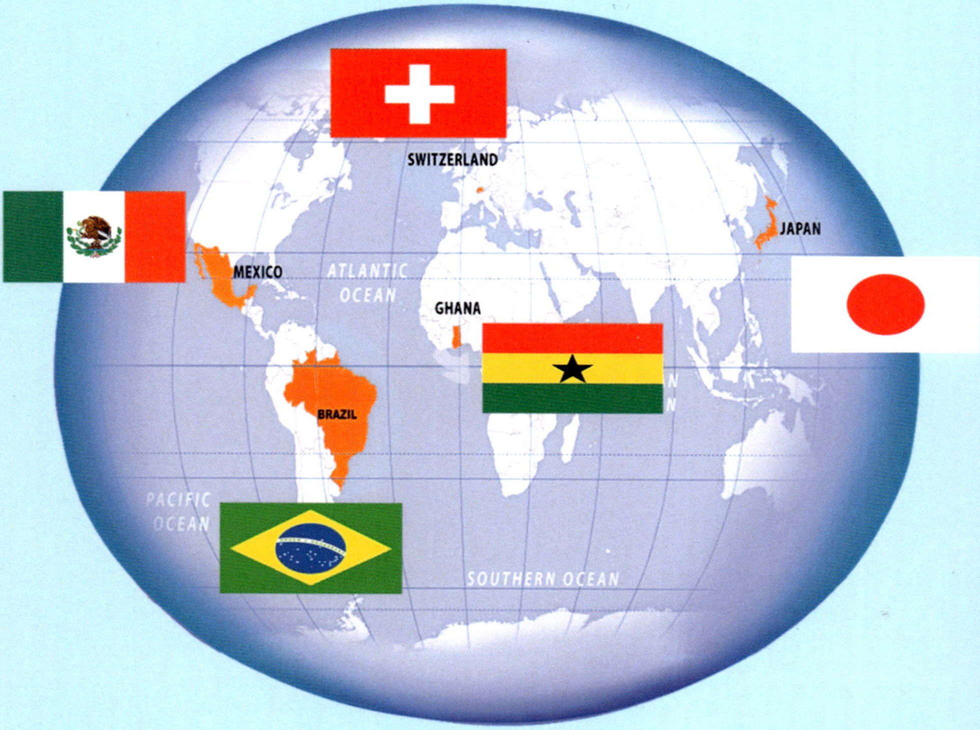

A Little Currency is an introduction to money around the world.

$9.9
ISBN 978-0-578-69280-
5099
9 780578 692807